MODERN RUSSIAN MASTERWORKS

DMITRI SHOSTAKOVICH

SONATA OPUS 147
FOR VIOLA AND PIANO

ISBN 978-0-79353-864-5

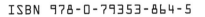

G. SCHIRMER, Inc.

DISTRIBUTED BY
HAL•LEONARD® CORPORATION
7777 W. BLUEMOUND RD. P.O. BOX 13819 MILWAUKEE, WI 53213

The Viola Sonata, the very last work composed by the great Russian master, Dmitri Shostakovitch, was written for Fyodor Druzhinin, a member of the Beethoven Quartet, to whom it was dedicated. It was first performed in Moscow on December 28, 1975 by Druzhinin and Mikhail Muntyan.

Sonata
for Viola and Piano

Dmitri Shostakovitch, Op. 147

I

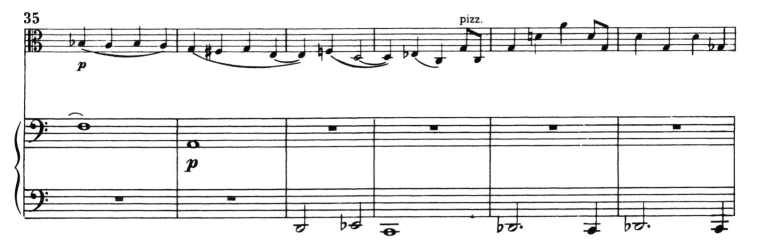

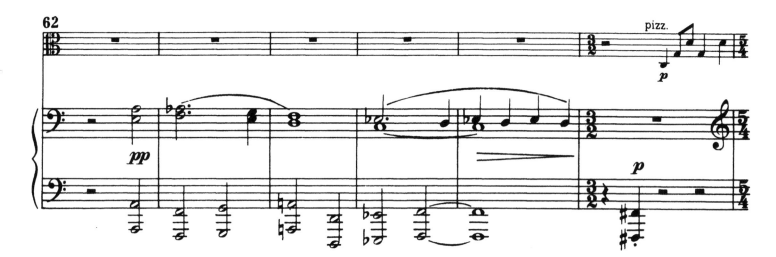

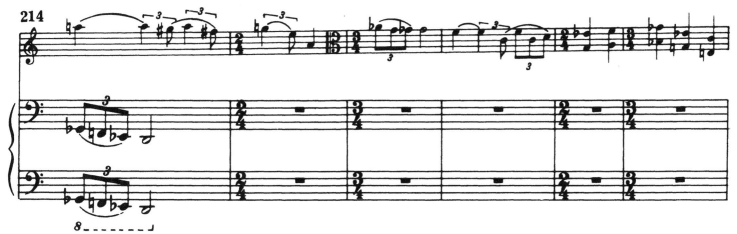

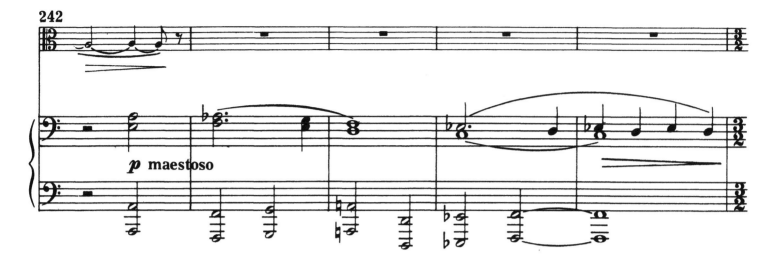

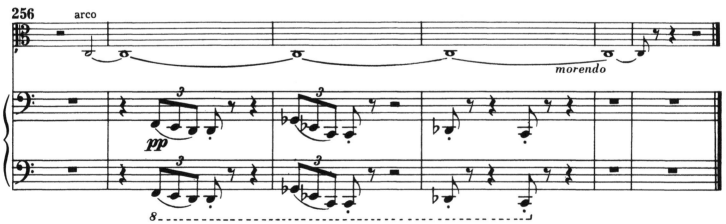

II

Viola

to Fjodor Drushinin
Sonata
for Viola and Piano

Dmitri Shostakovitch, Op. 147

I

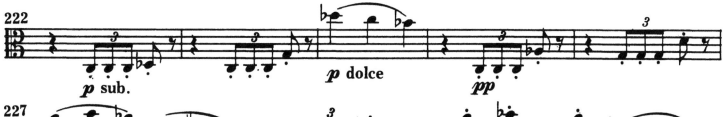

II

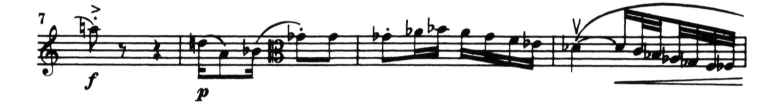

187

192

cresc.　　　　　　　　　　　　　　　　　　　　　　　　*ff*　　　*ff* espr.

194

198

p

204

209

217

222

ff

227

232

f espr.　　　　　　　　　　　　　　　　　　　　　　　　　　*p*

240

312

319

328

III

5

8

13

325

331

III

Adagio ♩ = 80

6

13

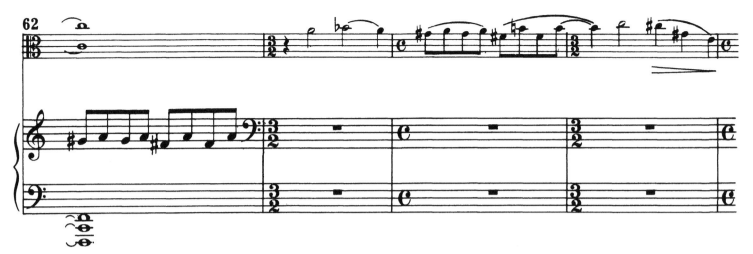

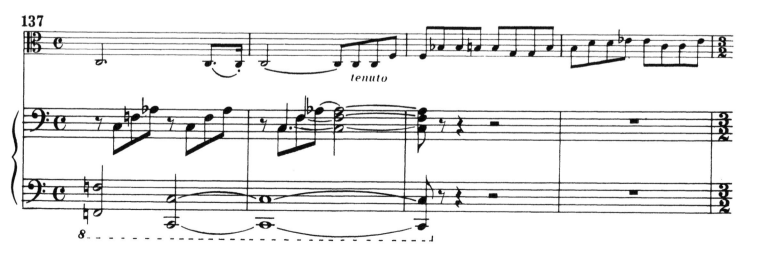

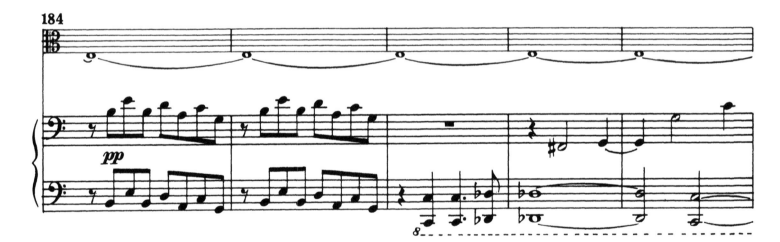

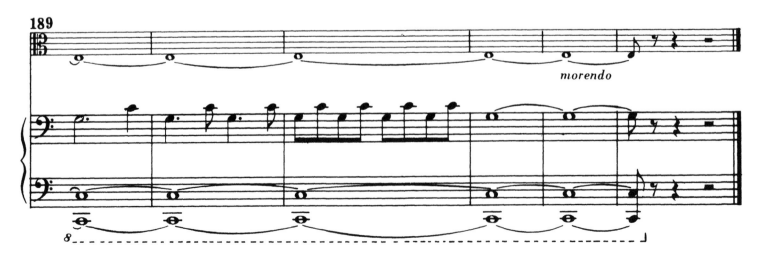